# THE FANTASTIC FLATULENT FART BROTHERS'

# BIG BOOK OF

# SNOTTY FACTS

## AN ILLUSTRATED GUIDE TO THE SCIENCE, HISTORY, AND PLEASURES OF MUCUS

## M.D. Whalen

illustrated by Florentino Gopez

## Publisher's Cataloging-in-Publication Data

Names: Whalen, M.D., author. | Gopez, Florentino, illustrator.
Title: The fantastic flatulent fart brothers' big book of snotty facts : an illustrated guide to the science , history , and pleasures of mucus / M.D. Whalen ; illustrated by Florentino Gopez.
Series: The Fantastic Flatulent Fart Brothers Fun Facts
Description: Silvermine Bay, Hong Kong: Top Floor Books, 2020.
Summary: Fifty entertaining but true facts about the science, history, and art of mucus, including fifty illustrations and famous quotes.
Identifiers: ISBN: 9789627866442 (pbk., USA) | 9789627866459 (pbk., UK) | 9789627866466 (ebook, USA) | 9789627866473 (ebook, UK)
Subjects: LCSH Mucus–Juvenile literature. | Respiration–Juvenile literature. | Body fluids–Juvenile literature. | Humour. | CYAC Mucus. | Respiration. | Body fluids. | BISAC JUVENILE NONFICTION / Humour / General | JUVENILE NONFICTION / Health & Daily Living / Bodily Functions
Classification: LCC QP215 .W43 2020 | DDC 612.2–dc23

ISBN 978 962 7866 45 9
First UK/international edition, published 2020

Top Floor Books
PO Box 29
Silvermine Bay, Hong Kong
topfloorbooks.com

# CONTENTS

# INTRODUCTION

HOW MUCH DO you know about snot?

Sure, it's gross. And people bigger than you are always telling you not to eat it. But mucus in all its forms is important to our bodies and is pretty fascinating stuff.

Did you know that snot is safe to eat? That we're not the only creatures who enjoy mining our noses? Robots have snot. Many powerful people pick it and lick it. Bogeys make both a good toothpaste and a shark repellent!

How much mucus do you swallow every day without knowing? What is most people's favourite picking finger? Why would you smear snail slime on your face? Who invented artificial snot...and why?

Stick your finger in these pages for a taste of the gooey and glorious world of bogeys, snot, sputum, and slime.

SECTION ONE

# What is Snot?

FIRST, LETS GET our gross words straight.

**Mucus:** The general scientific term for the slimy substance in your body, from the watery stuff to hard nuggets and everything in-between.

**Mucous membrane:** The part of your body that makes mucus. Did you notice a spelling issue? *Mucus* is the gooey stuff, while *mucous* (with an added O) is the gland which produces it. Why the different spellings? Because English is weird! Look on the bright side—we get two gross words in the dictionary instead of one.

**Phlegm:** Pronounced *flem,* it's the syrupy mucus filling your throat and lungs when you're sick.

**Sputum:** What phlegm becomes when you cough it into people's faces.

**Nasal detritus:** What scientists politely call mucus that's thick enough to be scooped by a finger. Normal people just call it...

**Snot:** Related to the word *snout,* this word has been used for over six hundred years, so keep tradition alive by using it.

**Bogey:** Harder and more chewy than snot.

Finally, a word we wish was more popular...

**Snite:** Blow your nose without paper or hankie. An old word now used mainly in Scotland. Is blowing your nose on your kilt still *sniting?*

# Snot Psychology

DO YOU PICK your nose every day? Then you might be a rhinotillexomaniac!

The scientific word for picking your nose is **rhinotillexis**. This comes from the ancient Greek word *rhinos,* meaning nose, which you *till*—that is, to scoop up soil with a shovel or hoe—toward the *exis,* which means exit. Together it becomes *rhino-till-exis:* nose-shovel-exit, or scooping out your nose.

Someone who constantly picks his or her nose is a nose-scooping-out maniac, better known as a **rhinotillexomaniac**. That's you.

Eating snot after you've picked—I mean *tillexized*—it is called **mucophagy**, from *mucus* and the ancient Greek word *phagy,* meaning eat. They couldn't just call it snot-gobbling.

Psychologists didn't stop there. Everyone has a weird uncle who plucks his nose hairs in front of you. This habit is **rhinotrichotillomania**. *Tricho* means hair, so: nose-hair-digging-crazy.

There's no word for eating nose hairs, though. Now, *that* would be gross!

# Snot Ingredients

THE STUFF IN your nose is more than ninety percent water and a bit of salt. It also contains:

3% mucins
0.5% proteoglycan
0.5% lipids
1% immunoglobulins, lysozymes, and albumin

**Mucins** are what make mucus thick and gooey and turn your nostrils into human flypaper, except to catch germs instead of bugs.

**Proteoglycan** is a super sticky kind of sugar molecule. Maybe it's the secret ingredient that gives snot its flavour.

**Lipids** are fats found in every cell in your body. Yes, you. Your cells are fat.

**Immunoglobulins** may sound like something you'd find in a haunted house, but they're more scary to the germs they kill in your mucus.

**Lysozymes** are enzymes which kill bacteria. They're also in your tears to protect your eyes.

**Albumin** is a thickener, same as in egg whites.

So, if a combination of flypaper glue, fat, globulins, tears, and raw eggs sounds delicious, then snot might be just the snack for you.

# What's the Point of Mucus?

MUCUS MAY BE gross, but it catches even grosser stuff like germs, dust, and animal hair to keep them out of your lungs.

Snot also helps your sense of smell. Tiny particles and chemicals in the air might shoot right past the smell receptors in your nose. Catching them in mucus gives the nose time to analyse them and alert your brain to possible dangers and delights.

Imagine if you missed smelling that fresh baked chocolate cake because you ate all your bogeys and there was nothing left to do its job!

But why is there so much of it sometimes?

**Cold or flu:** With more viruses inside you, your body pours on the mucus to flush them out.

**Allergy:** Your body is ejecting dust, pollen, or fur.

**Cold weather:** Blood vessels in your nose expand to warm the air before it reaches your lungs. That extra blood flow triggers more mucus, which often ends up on your mittens.

**Crying:** Some tears drain under your eyeballs right into the sinuses. There they water down your mucus, which dribbles out by the bucket.

It's about time snot got some respect!

# Snot Colour Guide

WONDER WHY SNOT comes in different colours? Smear some on this page and learn!

- **Clear:** Normal, healthy, boring mucus.
- **White:** Your snot is losing moisture because the air is dry. Drink something, quick. Other than your mucus, that is.
- **Yellow:** White blood cells are fighting germs in your lungs. The exhausted warriors turn yellow and are carried out in your mucus. You may have a cold or flu coming on.
- **Green:** Armies of white blood cells are at full-scale war with invading germs. But that isn't camouflage colours they're wearing. So many dead white cells turn your bogeys green. You are a sick puppy!
- **Brown:** You might have inhaled dust or pollution all day. Not a good idea to eat this.
- **Black:** Either you've breathed in heavy smoke or you're seriously ill. Do not ingest!
- **Bright red:** You have a nose bleed, silly. Have you been picking too hard?

Next time a doctor wants to check your health, tell her to stick a finger up your nose.

# The Sneeze Limit

WHAT'S MORE DANGEROUS, a sneeze or a hurricane?

A full-blown sneeze shoots up to 40,000 tiny mucus droplets into the air. Most of those drops are the width of a human hair, yet each can hold 5000 viruses. In other words, a single sneeze can send 200 million germs flying through the air. And we mean flying.

The fastest sneeze ever measured went 102 miles (164 km) per hour. In fact, a hearty sneeze has a wind speed faster than a category two hurricane, and a lot more germs and gooey glop.

# Bogey Beverage

YOUR SINUSES PRODUCE around two litres of fresh mucus every day. Where does all that goo go?

*You swallow it.*

That's right, you gulp down two litres of snot every day without realising it. The gooey stuff flows non-stop from your mucous membranes down toward your lungs, catching germs and dust along the way. Tiny hairs called cilia push the used phlegm up the back of your throat, where it joins snot sliding down the back of your nose.

Then you swallow it, whether you know it or not, over a hundred times a day.

If you think that's gross, well, it isn't. You'd die without swallowing your mucus.

Your stomach produces acid strong enough to dissolve food. What stops that acid from burning through the walls of your stomach and intestines? The mucus you swallow, which conveniently coats your guts.

So raise a glass of mucus! This round is on you!

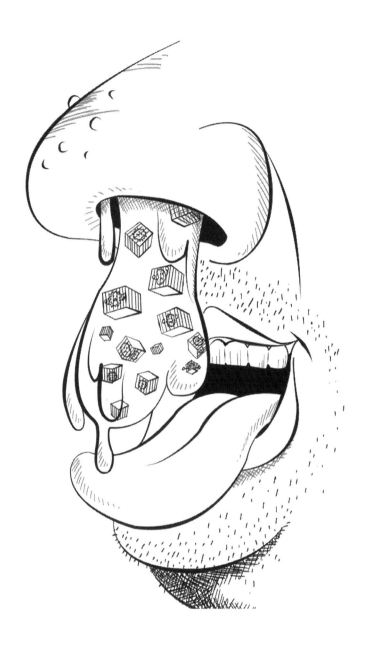

# Snot Health Food

IS IT SAFE to eat your bogeys?

We naturally swallow two litres of mucus every day. So, what difference will a few extra nose nuggets make?

Sure, snot is meant to trap germs, so it must be full of them. But it isn't that simple. Mucins—the stuff that makes mucus sticky—lock up bacteria and viruses and prevent them from growing and spreading. They're trapped in your snot.

According to doctors at the University of Kentucky, when you swallow your mucus, all those captive germs are killed by the digestive acids inside your stomach.

'Swallowing phlegm probably reduces the chance of spreading infection to those around you,' writes Dr. Laszlo Tamas. 'Eating your snot is safer than sneezing.'

Canadian biochemist Scott Napper goes even further. He says eating snot is good for you.

Professor Napper believes that snot tastes good for a reason. Maybe nature is encouraging you to eat it. Swallowing those trapped germs trains your immune system, just like vaccination, making your body stronger.

A bogey a day keeps the doctor away!

# Bogey
# Nutrition Facts

8 servings per nostril
**Serving size**        **1 finger (15 mL)**

**Amount Per Serving**
# Calories       3

**%Daily Value***

| | |
|---|---|
| **Total Fat** 1g | **1%** |
|   Saturated Fat 0g | **0%** |
|   *Trans* Fat 0g | |
| **Cholesterol** 0mg | **0%** |
| **Sodium** 1mg | **0%** |
| **Total Carbohydrate** 0mg | **0%** |
|   Dietary Fibre 0g | **0%** |
|   Total Sugars 0g | |
|     Includes 0g Added Sugars | **0%** |
| **Protein** 1g | |

| | |
|---|---|
| Vitamin C 3mg 3% | · Vitamin D 0mg 0% |
| Iron 500mcg 3% | · Calcium 0mg 0% |

**INGREDIENTS:**
Natural Mucus (water, mucin, proteoglycan, immunoglobulin. lipids, lysozome, albumin), salt, saliva (as a softening agent)

**ALLERGEN INFORMATION:**
May contain traces of nose hair, pollen, cat fur, carpet dust, tissue fibres, air freshener, dandruff, insect wings, smog, viruses, and whatever was on your finger.

100% organic, non-GMO, free range, gluten free, fair trade, no added colouring or flavouring

*The Percent Daily Value tells you how much a nutrient in a serving of snot contributes to a daily diet. Your daily value may vary depending on your calorie needs and the frequency that you pick your nose.

# Bogey Nutrition

SNOT IS MORE nutritious than you think.

One tablespoon of mucus contains around 3 calories, 1 milligram of salt, 1 gram of fat, and 500 milligrams of protein. There is even a little bit of vitamin C and iron.

The same amount of butter has 88 calories, 11 milligrams of salt, 10 grams of fat, and less than 100 milligrams of protein.

In other words, snot has fewer calories, less salt and fat, and more protein than butter. It's also organic, free range (unless you're in school or prison), gluten free, sugar free, fair trade, and not genetically modified. Plus, no colouring, flavouring, or wasteful packaging.

It gets better. The protein in mucus is called glycosylated protein, which is essential for a healthy brain and nerves. Snot makes you smarter!

For breakfast tomorrow, why not slather your toast with a layer of organic high-protein snot?

# Is Snot Vegan?

VEGANS DON'T EAT anything that comes from an animal—no meat, chicken, fish, eggs, milk, cheese, or even honey.

But what about eating your own snot?

Technically, snot is an animal product. Call it nose butter. Vegans don't eat butter. Therefore, many vegans claim they don't eat their snot.

Not everyone agrees. After all, harvesting your own bogeys doesn't hurt another creature. Unlike eggs or milk, you're not stealing it from an animal. It's yours! By that logic, snot makes a fine vegan snack.

But only if it's from your own nose. As the saying goes:

*You can pick your friends,*
*And you can pick your nose,*
*But you can't pick your friend's nose.*

Whoever wrote that must have been vegan.

# Snottiest Foods

EVERYONE KNOWS THAT dairy foods–like milk, cheese, and ice cream–give you lots of mucus. Except, that isn't true! Dairy foods make your phlegm thicker, but they don't make more of it.

But don't give up hope. If it's snot you want, the most phlegm-inducing things to eat are:

- Fried foods
- Red meat, like hamburgers and bacon
- Eggs
- Wheat, such as bread, spaghetti, and cakes
- Corn products, like tortilla chips
- Most breakfast cereals
- Potatoes, especially chips
- Cabbage
- Bananas
- Sodas and other sugary drinks

The prize for the snottiest food of all?

- *Soybeans!*

Soybeans also make you fart more than other beans. The perfect food!

So have a soy burger on a wheat bun with chips and a soda, and biscuits for pudding. You'll whip up so much snot it'll be like getting two meals for the price of one!

# Bird Spit Soup

NEXT TIME YOU visit a Chinese restaurant, try some bird's nest soup. Yes, it's made from real nests.

Chinese food lovers will tell you how tasty and healthy bird's nests are. What they don't tell you is what they're made from.

The soup is made from swift and swallow nests. These quick little birds don't build nests out of twigs and leaves like other birds. Instead, they spit out thick strings of phlegm which they weave into nests, then leave them to dry.

When boiled in water, the nests melt and turn into a thick broth, which is nothing more than re-hydrated bird spit.

Chefs also steam bird's nests into a hard jelly for pudding. Sounds tempting.

What about the health factor? Drinking bird's nest soup might be no more nutritious than eating your own snot, but at least no one will scold you for it.

# Snot Pudding

IN JAPAN THEY eat Gorilla Bogeys for pudding.

Not real gorilla bogeys. It's a sweet made by a Japanese company called Hanakuso, whose company name translates as 'Nose Poo'.

Gorilla Bogeys, made of black beans and sugar, come in little bags showing a cartoon gorilla picking its nose. If you're hungry for something cuter than ape snot, the Nose Poo company also offers Panda Snot, made of soy beans and sugar. Since soy beans and sugar give you lots of mucus, these come close to being actual snot.

If you want more heavenly food, you might pick The Great Buddha's Nose Snot. It's made of puffed rice and is supposed to bring you good luck. Buddhist leaders have tried to block its sale, and no wonder—the package shows a cartoon of Buddha picking his nose.

If the idea of eating animal bogeys or holy snot turns you off, you can always try a scoop of Deer Poop ice cream: green tea ice cream sprinkled with little brown pellets.

You'll never go hungry in Japan.

# SNOT HEALTH

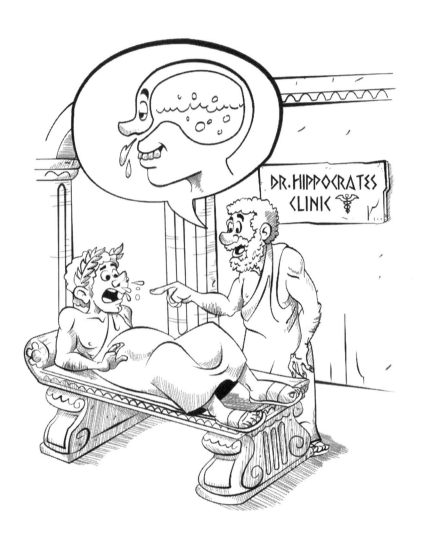

# Snot for Brains

ANCIENT GREEK DOCTORS believed that mucus came from your brain.

Around 400 BC, Hippocrates, known as the father of medicine, wrote that when people had runny noses it meant their brains were leaking out (it does feel like that sometimes). If someone was sad or forgetful, blame it on the bogeys.

Someone with a lot of phlegm was called phlegmatic (*fleg-MA-tick*), a word we still use today. It means someone who is sad and dull-minded and doesn't express their feelings.

Did Hippocrates stop and think that maybe people were sad and dull because they were dribbling snot all over their clean white togas? After all, tissue paper wasn't invented until a thousand years later way over in China.

He also didn't answer the most important question of all: if snot comes from your brain, does eating it make you smarter?

# SNOT Licence

IF YOU FEEL stuffy and congested, a doctor might make you fill out a special form with questions about your nose and mucus. This 22-question quiz is called:

Sino-Nasal Outcome Test

*Hint: spell out the first letter of each word.*

You got it! Yes, doctors and hospitals around the world will give you a SNOT exam. But only if they're licensed.

Just like you can only drive a car if you have a driver's licence, if a doctor or hospital wants to use this test on their patients, they have to buy a SNOT Licence. That's really what it's called.

You don't have to be a doctor to be licensed. Simply sign up at the official website and pay the fee.

Be the first person on your block to be licensed for SNOT!

# Hospital Bogeys

BIOLOGISTS AT THE Massachusetts Institute of Technology want to smear snot around hospitals.

Medical equipment collects many kinds of bacteria, which gather into thin, sticky layers called biofilms. These can become dangerously infectious and are often difficult to remove. The MIT scientists think mucus is the answer.

As we know, mucin, the stuff that makes mucus sticky, traps bacteria and stops them from growing.

These scientists suggest that if hospital and laboratory equipment is painted with a coat of mucin, it will keep bacteria apart, which will prevent biofilms from forming and stop infections from spreading.

Next time someone catches you wiping your bogeys on the the sofa, explain that you're protecting them from an epidemic.

Snot saves lives!

# Snot Toothpaste

MOST PEOPLE CLEAN their mouths with toothpaste, floss, and mouthwash. Why bother, when you can simply smear snot on your teeth?

A study published by the American Society for Microbiology suggests that mucus would make a good toothpaste. Mucus proteins called mucins trap bacteria, so they can't stick to your teeth. If they don't stay on your teeth, then they won't cause cavities.

The study's authors do not suggest rubbing bogeys on your teeth instead of brushing. They believe that synthetic mucus made in laboratories can offer the same protection.

And a whole new world of toothpaste flavours.

42

# Humming for Health

IF YOU'RE CONGESTED and coughing from a throat full of phlegm, you might take cold medicine, sip hot lemon tea, or go through every box of tissues in the house.

Or you could hum a tune.

Our sinuses make more than just mucus. They also produce a gas called nitric oxide (NO). This is a good thing. When you inhale nitric oxide, it relaxes your lungs, which is helpful when you have a cold or other breathing problem.

Your skull bones vibrate when you hum. Researchers in Sweden discovered that these vibrations stimulate your sinuses into pumping out more nitric oxide. When you hum, you send twenty-four times more of this soothing gas into your lungs.

As Winnie-the-Pooh says, 'Hums aren't things which you get, they're things which get you.' It seems that they cure you, too.

If you can't think of anything to hum, try 'The Nose Pickin' Song' near the end of this book.

44

# Big Nose Picker

'PICKING YOUR NOSE will make your nose bigger.' This is one way that grownups try to frighten kids into pulling their finger out.

Picking your nose might not win you a beauty contest, but will it really make your nose gross and deformed? Let's ask a doctor.

Dr Shervin Naderi is the only surgeon in the United States who operates exclusively on human noses, so he 'nose' what he's talking about. Dr Naderi says that frequent nose picking might stretch the skin a little, but you would have to pick from morning until night for months and months before you see any change.

Anyway, even the most enthusiastic poking and scooping doesn't produce enough force to affect the bone and cartilage which create your nose's shape.

Anyone who claims that nose picking turns you ugly can go poke it...up their nose!

# Death by Bogey

WHAT HAPPENED TO poor Ian Bothwell should send a shiver up your nose.

Mr Bothwell, who lived alone in Manchester, England, was found dead on the floor beside his bed. The doctor who examined the body said he died from picking his nose:

'The nasal cavity was filled with blood. My conclusion is that the most likely cause of death is epistaxis, the technical term for a nose bleed. The most common cause of epistaxis is picking the nose and I believe that is likely to be what happened.'

In other words, Ian picked so much that his nose bled. When he lay down to sleep, blood ran down his throat and choked him.

The Manchester coroner closed the case: 'There is no explanation for this death other than he died from a nose bleed, consistent with picking his nose.'

Let that be a warning: never pick your nose before bed.

# SNOTTY ANIMALS

# Dinosaur Snot

TYRANNOSAURUS REX HAD big teeth and tiny hands, but more important: what about its snot? American paleontologist Lawrence Witmer was determined to find out.

T-Rex had enormous sinuses which made its skull lighter and could hold enough mucus to fill a small bathtub. Poor T-Rex! Its arms were too short to pick its nose for this treasure. But how much came out when it sneezed?

Professor Witmer and his students designed an experiment to discover the truth. They built a computerised model based on what they knew about T-Rex sinuses, lungs, and throats. Then they imitated a dinosaur-sized prehistoric sneeze.

Seven gallons, or twenty-seven litres.

That's how much dino-snot a T-Rex might sneeze in your face. Though if you came that close to a stuffy-nosed meat-eating dinosaur, a splash of sputum on your cheeks would be the last thing you'd worry about.

# Ape Snot

*Q: Why do gorillas have such big nostrils?*
*A: Have you seen the size of those fingers?*

THERE'S SOME TRUTH to the joke.

Apes blow their noses all the time. Some press a nostril shut and blast snot from the other.

Others use tools. African chimpanzees and South American capuchin monkeys poke sticks into their noses—not to collect bogeys, but to trigger a sneeze to clear things out.

Gorillas have a problem. Their nostrils face forward, so you can imagine which way a sneeze would fly—right into their friend's face! Plus, those nostrils are pretty big, so they hold quite a feast. That's why gorillas pick their noses with their big fat fingers and, while they're at it, they often taste test the product.

But the ape snot prize goes to bonobos, who live in Africa and are related to chimpanzees. When their babies get runny noses, mother bonobos use their lips to suck the snot out.

Bet you wish you had a mum like that.

# Giraffe Snot

A GIRAFFE'S NECK isn't the only thing that's extra-long. Its tongue can stick out around one and a half feet, almost half a metre.

Mostly they use their flexible tongues to pluck leaves from acacia trees, their favorite food. But a giraffe's tongue can gather another tasty snack. You guessed it...

If giraffes are feeling a bit stuffy, they blow their upward-facing nostrils just hard enough to move snot into the opening. Then their tongue reaches inside and performs a house cleaning.

A bit of giraffe bogey salad cream for your acacia leaf salad, anyone?

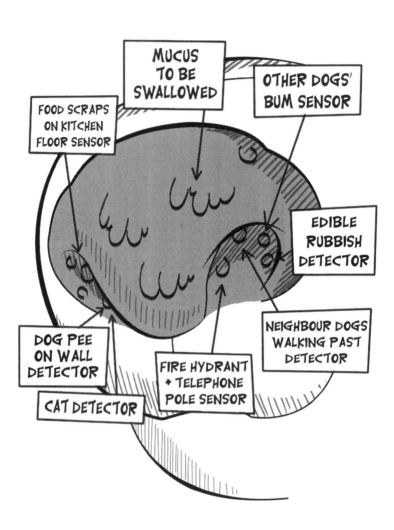

# Dog Snot

DOGS SWALLOW THEIR own snot, for a good reason.

The moisture on a healthy dog's nose is actually a thin layer of clear mucus. It helps your pup's sense of smell.

Dogs' noses are thousands of times more sensitive than people's. They have over 100 million scent receptors in their nostrils, compared to 6 million in humans, plus a larger part of their brain is devoted to analysing smells. But their real trick is a special olfactory gland on the roof of a dog's mouth called Jacobsen's organ.

The slimy film on their nose absorbs odours and chemicals in the air which their smell receptors might not catch. When a dog licks its nose, it brings the mucus inside where the Jacobsen's organ can study it closely. It's like having a second nose, only this one smells its own snot.

Wolves have wet noses for the same reason. The better to smell you with, my dear!

# Whale Snot

'THAR SHE BLOWS!' went the old sailor's cry when spotting a whale. Nowadays those words have a new meaning.

In 2015 the Ocean Alliance, an environmental organisation, was observing whales out at sea. A whale surfaced nearby and blew a huge blast from its blowhole, showering everyone on board with slimy whale spit.

The researchers were delighted!

A whale blow is similar to a sneeze: full of phlegm which scientists study to learn about their health, diet, and DNA.

The expedition leader reported, 'This whale snot sort of pummeled over my body. As you can imagine, from a biologist's perspective the stinkier it is, the more gross it is, typically the more productive and more interesting it is.'

But getting close enough to collect the gooey stuff is dangerous.

So the scientists created drone copters to fly over whales and collect their spit. They named this important invention Snotbots.

Sorry, you can't buy a Snotbot for yourself, but you can get an official Snotbot hoodie to protect yourself in case a whale surfaces nearby.

# Escar-goo

THE ANCIENT GREEKS invented democracy, geometry, and the Olympics. They also invented smearing snail slime on your face.

Greek doctors treated skin problems by rubbing on snail slime. They cured stomach aches by making patients drink the stuff. If that made them choke, then swallow even more. The Greeks also made cough syrup out of snail goo.

Two thousand years later, farmers in Chile noticed that skin cuts healed quickly and their hands felt smoother whenever they handled snails. They switched to snail farming, turning snail slime into skin creams.

Studies confirm that snail mucus heals and softens damaged skin. It even clears up acne.

Nowadays, snail slime beauty cream is a huge business in Korea. In beauty spas in Thailand, snails do the work by crawling on customers' faces.

The best slime comes from the Brown Garden Snail, like the ones in your garden. Who needs soap to clean your face when snails can do it for you?

# Sea Snot Shooters

SPIDER-MAN MAY BE cool, but he's no match for the slimy superpowers of the worm snail.

Soon after they're born, these sea-dwelling molluscs attach themselves to nearby rocks or coral and are stuck there for life. It's tough to go out to eat when you're glued to a rock, so worm snails came up with a sticky solution—they hunt for food with their phlegm.

Extra tentacles near their bottoms are actually slime-shooting guns. The worm snail blasts out bands of mucus which form into a sticky web, much like a spider's. Tiny creatures get caught in the strings. When it's time for supper, the worm snail sucks it all in.

Microscopic villains beware: here comes your friendly neighbourhood Wormsnail-Man!

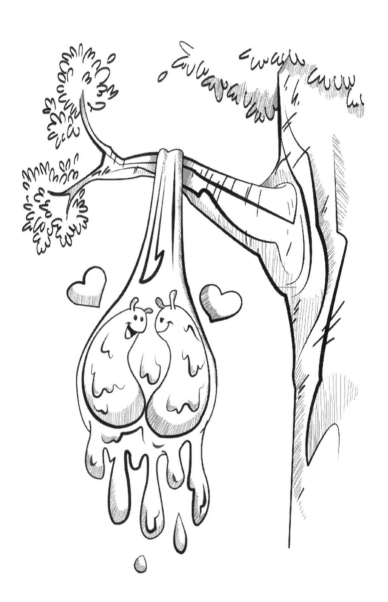

# Romantic Slug Snot

IF A SLUG goes out on a date, being called a slimeball is a compliment.

When they're in the mood for love, romantic young slugs climb onto a nearby tree or bush and ooze gooey mucus all over each other. Encased in this jelly-like mass, they drop from the branch and dangle in the air on a sticky thread of slime and do a slow circle dance of love.

When it's all over, they eat the mucus off each other's bodies. Then they climb back up the slime rope and go their separate ways.

Cheaper than going out to dinner and a movie.

# Frog Snot Medicine

THE MUCUS OF a colourful, fist-sized frog from the jungles of India could hold the cure to the flu.

The charmingly named Widespread Fungoid Frog is an eye-catching orange, black, and yellow. A chemical in its mucus can destroy many kinds of influenza viruses.

But don't start sucking down frog bogeys when you're sick. Other elements in Fungoid Frog snot are poisonous to people. Chemists are working on ways to remove the bad parts.

Someday, eating frog snot might save your life.

# Sneeziest Animals

MOST ANIMALS SNEEZE, even fish. But which animal would win the Olympic sneezing competition?

**Bronze Medal for Grossest Sneeze** goes to seals and sea lions. According to biologist Julie Avery, these blubbery sea mammals not only constantly snort out gluey snot, but they like to 'hock loogies which go quite a distance.'

The **Silver Medal for Loudest Sneeze** is awarded to elephants. Think of how much force is needed for a sneeze to travel the length of their trunk. John Lenhart of the National Elephant Center says an elephant sneeze 'can be very loud, as you might imagine, and is usually accompanied by a significant spray also. It is normal, but just elephant-sized.'

And the **Gold Medal for Sneeziest Animal** goes to...*iguanas!* These tough lizards rid their bodies of excess salt by constantly sneezing out snalt all day. Yes, *snalt*. That's what iguana experts call the thick, salty snot that shoots out an iguana's nose.

Snalt is nasty stuff that can eat through steel and brass, another reason iguanas get the corrosion-proof gold.

Bless you, iguanas!

# THE ART OF NOSE PICKING

# Snot Polite

IN MEDIEVAL EUROPE, blowing your nose into your hand, even at meals, was considered perfectly polite, but with one condition. According to a German guide to good behaviour:

*Do not blow your nose with the same hand that you use to hold the meat.*

Or as long as you didn't eat it *instead* of the meat. A French book of manners warned:

*It is very impolite to put what you have pulled from your nose into your mouth.*

In other words, no problem pulling stuff from your nose—just don't swallow it.

In the 1400s someone finally invented the idea of blowing your nose into a cloth. But handkerchiefs were ridiculously expensive. Many rich people showed off their wealth by carrying handkerchiefs between their teeth.

If people were too poor for a hankie, what did they use? We get a clue from the Dutch philosopher Erasmus, who penned this warning:

*To blow your nose on your hat is rude.*

Not to mention that it would get in your hair!

# Snot Statistics

HOW DO MOST people pick their noses? Yes, scientists actually study this stuff! According to a report in the *Journal of Psychiatry*:

- 91% of adults regularly pick their noses
- 55.5% pick bogeys 1 to 5 minutes a day
- 23.5% pick between 5 and 15 minutes a day
- 8.7% claim they've never picked a nose in their life. Do you believe them?

Which finger do people prefer?

- 65.1% use their index finger
- 20.2% use their little finger
- 16.4% use their thumb
- 9 people claimed they pick their nose with a pencil. *Ouch!*

What do they do with the snot?

- 90.3% wipe it off with a tissue or cloth
- 7.6% smear it on furniture
- Only 8% admit to ever eating the product

If you are one of the 92 percent who claim you've never picked your nose or eaten snot... yeah, right! A study at the University of Massachusetts proves that most people tell at least one lie every day.

DECOY HEADACHE

THE HAIR WIPE

PICK -N- FLICK

PICK -N- STICK

# Picking in Public

SOMETIMES YOU FEEL a wad stuck way up inside and you just *have* to scoop it out with other people around. How many of these secret nose picking techniques have you tried?

**The Itch:** Make believe your nose itches, while actually plucking low-hanging bogeys.

**The Pinch:** Squeeze the nose like toothpaste and flick the result onto other people's shoes.

**Decoy Headache:** Cover your nose and pretend to massage a headache while slipping a finger inside. Fools them every time.

**The Turn-Around:** Turn to look at something across the room and do a split-second scoop.

**The Hair Wipe:** Pick with a moving hand, then pretend to brush hair from your eye. Deposit the prize behind your ear.

**Pick 'n Save:** A quick pick when your boss looks away, then wipe clean inside your pocket.

**Pick 'n Roll:** You know what I'm talking about.

**Pick 'n Flick:** Ditto.

**Pick 'n Stick:** Flick which sticks to your finger.

**Autopick:** Done in a car when nobody is looking.

**Pick Your Brains:** Your finger goes in so far, it disappears. Maybe not so good in public.

If you answered 5 or more, you're a Nose Master!

# HISTORICAL BOGEYS

# Gross Grave

PHILIP THE BOLD was a powerful prince in Medieval France. He must have had a powerful sense of humour.

Before he died in 1404, he hired sculptors to build him a tomb out of marble, surrounded by statues of angels, knights, lions, and forty-one mourners.

Two of them show their feelings by blowing their noses.

One clearly wipes his nose on his robe. Another wrings out his snout with his hand.

When he saw those statues, Philip must have died laughing!

# Napoleon Bogeypart

EMPEROR NAPOLEON MAY have been defeated at the Battle of Waterloo. But one fight he never gave up was the Battle of the Bogey.

Napoleon's fingers never stopped invading his nostrils, according to several eyewitnesses. As one church goer wrote, Napoleon 'picked his nose very much', right in the middle of mass in a Paris chapel.

The makers of Bugs Bunny cartoons knew their history. In the 1956 cartoon, 'Napoleon Bunny-part', the snot-snacking emperor sticks a finger in not once, but twice.

No wonder Napoleon is always shown with a hand inside his vest. What better place to hide snotty fingers?

84

# Minister Mucus

GREAT BRITAIN WAS once a leading naval power. Now they're the leading nasal power.

In 2007, the future Prime Minister Gordon Brown was filmed in Parliament sticking a finger up both nostrils, then licking it before wiping it on his tie.

Too refined to soil his tie, in 2020 Labour Party leader Jeremy Corbyn was caught on camera in the House of Commons picking his nose and wiping the stuff on his beard.

But Labour doesn't have the nose picking monopoly in Parliament. In 2019, Conservative MP Iain Duncan Smith caused an uproar during a Brexit debate by thoroughly dipping a finger in his nostril. And then eating it.

Are bipartisan bogeys a taste of things to come in the United Kingdom?

# Her Royal Sinus

EVEN THE QUEEN of England can't resist sliding a finger into the royal proboscis.

As one would expect, Her Majesty doesn't pick like a mere commoner. She inserts an air of nobility by occasionally picking her nose with her gloves on.

The Queen isn't alone among royals bestowing one-finger knighthoods to their nostrils. Willem-Alexander, Crown Prince of the Netherlands, deserves the Olympic Gold Medal for Nose Picking.

At the Beijing Olympics in 2000, he thought all eyes were on the swimmers. Meanwhile, all cameras were on his nose and finger instead. The prince's nasal acrobatics included pinky finger deep diving and synchronized strokes with his thumb and forefinger.

Long may their royal noses run!

# Synthetic Snot

WOULD YOU EAT fake snot?

In 2006 a company in Oregon invented a new product called Boogerettes (based on the American spelling). They described it as an 'anti-nose picking therapeutic training device. Namely, manipulative synthetic dried nasal mucus.'

In other words, artificial bogeys.

The idea is that if chew on the stuff it will offer the satisfying feel of real snot and you'll quit the repulsive habit of scooping it from your nose.

Not surprisingly, they never made it into shops. Who needs fake when the real thing is free?

# Snot Swimsuit

THE HAGFISH, ALSO known as the slime eel, is the grossest creature beneath the ocean waves.

When a hagfish feels threatened, it spews out a sticky substance which expands into a big, thick wad of mucus. Kind of like when an octopus squirts a cloud of ink, except this is a cloud of snot that suffocates anything caught inside.

Some American Navy researchers thought hagfish snot was so cool they wanted to make it themselves. This turned out to be quite simple. It's actually just two proteins put out by the fish. When combined with seawater, it quickly turns into a jelly which expands ten thousand times in a fraction of a second.

Navy scientists think that artificial hagfish slime could be a cheap but powerful product to keep barnacles off ship hulls and to protect divers against sharks.

Don't forget to pack your fish snot next time you go to the beach!

# Robo-Bogeys

ROBOTS SMELL. YES, really. Electronic smell-sensing devices detect dangerous gases in factories and laboratories, track air pollution, monitor food for spoilage, assist police, and many other uses.

For now, robot noses are nowhere close to replacing the real odour experts: dogs. Our canine friends have over 300 million smell sensors in their noses. The best e-noses contain only fifty.

Researchers in England are closing that gap... with robot snot.

Dog mucus collects odours and makes their noses even more sensitive (see 'Dog Snot'). Engineers adapted the idea to e-noses.

They developed artificial mucus to spread on electronic sensors, which greatly increases their smelling power. Snot-enhanced robots can accurately tell apart safe and dangerous chemical odours. In China they even created a robot that can tell which person in a room farted.

Next they need to program robots to keep their fingers out of their cyber-noses.

# SNOT AROUND THE WORLD

# Nose Picking Day

FOR CHRISTMAS PEOPLE hand out presents. On Valentine's Day you give sweets and hearts.

What do you give someone for International Nose Picking Day?

Falling on April 23 each year, it's the one day you can proudly pick your nose in public. No tissues or handkerchiefs allowed.

So mark International Nose Picking Day on your calendar, and give a one-finger salute to the freedom to pick.

Just don't confuse it with National Nose Hair Maintenance Day: every September 8.

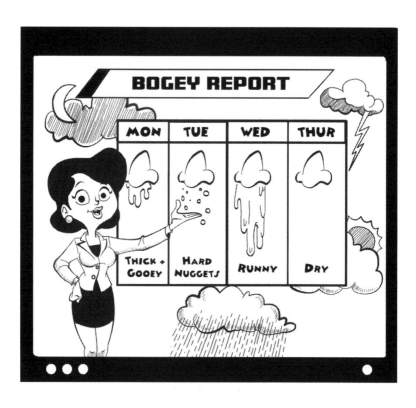

100

# Nose Climate

WHEN YOU PLAN a vacation, do you ever wonder, 'What will my bogeys be like?' Maybe you should.

Clean environments which are not too humid or too dry promote just enough mucus to do its job. But when you dig around, you get little reward. If that sounds boring...

Damp or humid places like the Amazon Jungle or New Orleans produce a stickier goo in greater volume, but it needs multiple finger scoops to get out.

Deserts and high plains are the best places for the serious snot lover. Arid climates dry out your nose, creating hard and rubbery nuggets, the favorite of snot connoisseurs for their satisfying chew.

Air quality also makes a difference. On days of heavy pollution, your sinuses work hard and produce big snotty chunks that are easy to pull out. But considering what they absorbed from the air, they might not make the healthiest travel snack.

So if it's a snot holiday you want, make sure to let yourself be led by the nose!

# Blowing It in Europe

EUROPEAN COUNTRIES HAVE fought wars for centuries. And no wonder–they can't even agree on how to blow their noses!

When in Rome, do as the Romans do: blow your nose anywhere. **Italy** is the home of opera, so it's no wonder that Italians happily serenade the world with the sound of mucus.

In **Germany**, even teachers blow their noses in front of a full classroom.

But keep your snot to yourself in **France**, where public nose blowing is considered a sign of bad upbringing.

In **Sweden**, people excuse themselves from class or work to clear their noses in private.

Same in snot-deprived **Iceland**, where geysers are allowed to blow in public, but people aren't.

Only **England** offers a compromise in the Euro-Snot War. William Hanson, England's leading etiquette coach instructs:

'One sniff is fine, two sniffs is unfortunate.'

Three snorts for England!

# Blowing It in Asia

IN CHINA, PEOPLE think it's the most disgusting thing they've ever seen when you blow your nose into a handkerchief, then shove the gooey cloth back into your pocket or purse. And even worse: re-use it later! It truly is gross if you think about it.

Use paper tissues instead? Not so fast. In **Vietnam** and **Cambodia**, blowing your nose anywhere in public is as rude as farting out loud, but without the laughter.

Don't even think about using your fingers. In **Thailand** it's rude to blow your nose or lick your fingers at meal time. So it must be extra rude to blow your nose and *then* lick your fingers.

Most sensitive of all is **Japan**, where even the slightest little sniff will earn you dirty looks, even in a public loo. This is a country that has musical toilet seats so people won't hear you pee. If you must expel snot, hide in a closed toilet booth, whistle a tune, and honk to the beat.

At least they give you some leeway in **India**. Blowing your nose in a classroom or office is a definite no-no. But you can get away with emergency sniffing until you reach a private place for a full-powered blow.

# Nose Picking Tours

WANT A HOLIDAY where nose picking is part of the fun? Visit Easter Island.

Actually, don't. The local people don't want you.

Easter Island, also called Rapa Nui, is a small island in the Pacific Ocean which is famous for giant stone heads carved by native islanders hundreds of years ago.

The island used to be hard to get to. People paid big money to travel by ship to this unique place. Most visitors treated the statues with respect.

Nowadays, with cheap flights, Rapa Nui receives thousands of tourists clutching selfie sticks, who pose with their fingers up ancient stone nostrils for 'amusing' social media feeds.

Funny, right? The people of Rapa Nui don't think so. They're starting to limit the number of visitors allowed on the island.

Next time you're on holiday, try to control yourself and stick to picking your own nose.

SECTION NINE

# SNOT ENTERTAINMENT

# Scientist Snot Jokes

ONE OF THE most respected scientists in history was forced to tell snot jokes on TV.

In 2017, the world-famous physicist Stephen Hawking appeared on Red Nose Day, a charity event to help poor people which was broadcast around the world. The joke they made him say?

'Hi, I'm Nose-it-all. Snot looking good.'

That's the best they could come up with for such a brilliant mind as Professor Hawking? No wonder he complained afterward:

'I am a world-renowned scientist who has shaped our understanding of the universe. And I'm being asked to make snot jokes.'

# Superstar Snot

HOW MUCH WOULD you pay for movie star snot?

During a late night television appearance in 2008, actress Scarlett Johansson kept sniffing back a runny nose. She complained that she'd caught a cold from another movie actor, Samuel L. Jackson.

The talk show's host Jay Leno perked up and handed her a tissue, and joked that the snot of two cinema stars combined had 'value'.

It turned out to be no joke. The actress blew her nose into the tissue and held it up to the camera, saying, 'You got some lipstick. And snot!' Then she dropped it into a plastic bag, signed the bag, and auctioned it on eBay.

It fetched £4300. Possibly the most expensive bogey in history.

The money went to a charity to feed hungry people. They might have lost their appetites if they knew how their meals were paid for.

Get a printable copy of the sheet music at fartboys.com/snotsong

# The Nose Pickin' Song

*Everybody's doin' it, doin' it, doin' it,*
*Pickin' their nose and chewin' it, chewin' it.*
*Put it in the oven and what do ya got?*
*Hot snot chocolate with a bogey on top!*
*Is it candy? No, it snot.*
*Everybody's doin' it now!*

ONE OF THE biggest hit songs in the year 1912 was 'Everybody's Doin' It Now' by the popular songwriter Irving Berlin.

No, he didn't write a tune about nose picking. It was actually an upbeat love song. Bratty little boys changed the words sometime in the 1940s and *The Nose Pickin' Song* is now more famous than the original.

It could have been worse. Imagine if they'd snotted up the lyrics to Irving Berlin's later hits, 'White Christmas' and 'God Bless America'.

# STOP PICKING!

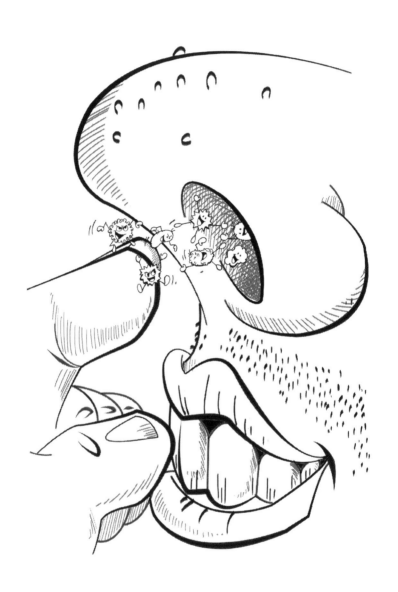

# It Really Is Gross

IS IT CRAZY to pick your nose? The American Psychological Association says no. They report that nose picking is not a mental problem.

That doesn't let you off the hook.

Sure, snot traps and kills germs, and is not a danger to your health.

Not even that lets you off the hook.

The biggest danger from picking your nose is not from eating snot, but from damaging your nostrils. A fingernail can scrape the sensitive lining of your nose, leaving gashes for germs to invade. If your sinus becomes infected, bacteria and viruses can eat into your skull, opening a doorway for them to march straight into your brain.

Where do those germs come from? Look no farther than under your fingernails. There lurks a nasty microbe called Staphylococcus aureus, which can cause pus-filled lumps inside your nose and spread throughout your body.

Did you just pet your dog or open a public loo door or grab a grimy escalator handrail? And then you stuck a finger up your nose?

It isn't the snot that's gross.

# How to Stop

PEOPLE HAVE TRIED to find a cure for nose picking for hundreds of years. Here are some popular suggestions.

- **Wear gloves or mittens.** That doesn't stop Queen Elizabeth (see page 87).
- **Put a bandage on your picking finger.** Does anyone use just one finger for the job?
- **Rinse your nostrils with salt water spray**, so there's nothing left to pick. Really? What's more gross—picking in public, or sitting in class with a spray bottle up your nose?
- **Wear an elastic band around your wrist.** Snap it when you feel the urge to pick. This is a great way to get snot all over your wrist, because most people don't realise they're picking their nose until their finger is halfway in.
- **See a psychiatrist.** Want to bet he picks his nose in private?

Only one piece of advice seems to work:

- **Ignore it!** Do it in private and no one will find out. Wash your hands frequently and keep your nails short.

HAPPY PICKING!

SECTION ELEVEN

BOGEY JOKES

# Bogey Jokes

You can pick your friends, and you can pick your nose, but you can't pick your friend's nose.

You can pick your friends, and you can pick your nose, but you can't wipe your friends off on the sofa.

If you were a bogey, I'd pick you first.

Some people say they pick their nose, but I was born with mine.

Your nose can run, but it can't hide.

What's the difference between snot and broccoli?
*Kids don't eat broccoli.*

What's the difference between plates and bogeys?
*Plates are on the table, but bogeys are under the table.*

What's the difference between a prince and a bogey?
*A prince is heir to the throne, but a bogey is thrown to the air.*

Whats the difference between a bucket of sand
and a bucket of snot ?
*You can't eat a bucket of sand.*

Why did the man catch his nose?
*Because it was running.*

What did the snot say to the nose?
*I gotta run.*

What does a bogey in love tell his girlfriend?
*I'm stuck on you.*

Why did the bogey cross the road?
*Because everyone was picking on him.*

How much does the average bogey weigh?
*Snot much.*

What's another name for a snail?
*A bogey wearing a crash helmet.*

What's your favourite type of bogey?
*It's hard for me to put my finger on just one.*

What's your favourite type of bogey?
*I can't remember...but it's on the tip of my tongue.*

Why was the nose sad?
*Because it didn't get picked!*

What do you find in a well-cleaned nose?
*Fingerprints!*

What did one bogey say to the other?
*Run for the hills, the fingers are coming!*

What's in a ghost's nose?
*Boo-geys.*

What do cows call their snot?
*Moo-cus.*

What do you call a pig's dried snot?
*A ham bogey!*

What did the bogey say to the finger?
*Pick on someone your own size.*

How did you know I went to Harvard?
*I noticed your class ring when you picked your nose.*

AN AUTO WORKER storms into his union leader's office and shouts, 'I have a pesky bogey in my nostril, and my bosses won't get us any more tissue boxes!!'

The union manager calmly responds, 'Maybe you should picket.'

A MAN WENT into a restaurant and ordered a bowl of soup. The waitress brought his order on a tray with her middle finger immersed in his soup bowl.

'What the heck's the idea of putting your finger in my soup bowl?' the man screamed at the waitress.

'My doctor said the best thing for my rheumatism is to keep my finger pressed in a warm damp place,' the waitress said.

'Oh yeah?' the man shouted. 'Then why don't you take that finger and of yours and thrust it in your nose?'

'I'm sorry sir,' the waitress replied, 'but I already tried that before I brought out your soup.'

# Bogey Poetry

Always eat your bogeys,
Don't wipe them on your clothes,
Just gulp them down in one
As you pick them from your nose.
For they're full of crunchy goodness,
They're best when green and long,
So always eat your bogeys
And you'll grow up big and strong.

# Bogey Quotes

It's not how you pick your nose, it's where you put the bogey that counts.
~ Tre Cool, musician

I guarantee you that Moses was a picker. You wander through the desert for forty years with that dry air. You telling me you're not going to have occasion to clean house a little bit?
~ Jerry Seinfeld, comedian

Love is like a bogey, you pick and pick at it. Then when you get it you wonder how to get rid of it.
~ Mae West, actress

He was the kind of kid you did not want to sit by. He kept his bogeys in his desk, he wore a neck tie.
~ John Hiatt, singer

Keep your nose to the grindstone. It sharpens your bogeys.
~ Steven Tyler, singer

Clouds are like bogeys hanging on the nostrils of the moon.
~ Robin Williams, actor

# References

What is Snot?
*europepmc.org/article/med/19166889*

*wikipedia.org/wiki/Mucus*

Snot Psychology
*psychologytoday.com/us/blog/in-excess/201401/snot-my-fault*

Snot Ingredients
*wikipedia.org/wiki/Mucus*

What's the Point of Mucus?
*kidshealth.org/en/kids/nose-run.html*

Snot Colour Guide
*health.clevelandclinic.org/2017/06/what-the-color-of-your-snot-really-means*

The Sneeze Limit
*livescience.com/3686-gross-science-cough-sneeze.html*

*ncbi.nlm.nih.gov/books/NBK143281/*

Bogey Beverage
*healthline.com/health/where-does-snot-come-from*

Snot Health Food
*journals.plos.org/plosone/article?id=10.1371/journal.pone.0209151*

*sciencemag.org/news/2016/07/new-antibiotic-found-human-nose*

*cbsnews.com/news/eating-boogers-may-boost-immunity-scientist-suspects*

Bogey Nutrition
*coolefitness.com/number-of-calories-in-boogers*

Is Snot Vegan?
*reddit.com/r/NoStupidQuestions/comments/acsmsv/is_eating_mucus_vegan*

Snottiest Foods
*livescience.com/63517-milk-does-not-create-mucus.html*

*lunginstitute.com/blog/21-foods-trigger-mucus-production-21-foods-reduce*

Bird Spit Soup
*wikipedia.org/wiki/Edible_bird's_nest*

Snot Pudding
*maki.typepad.com/justhungry/2009/11/the-great-buddhas-nose-snot.html*

*telegraph.co.uk/news/worldnews/asia/japan/1461852/Buddha-sweet-has-sour-taste-in-Japan.html*

*soranews24.com/2019/05/30/lets-try-some-deer-poop-ice-cream-in-nara-japans-city-of-deer*

Snot for Brains
*wikipedia.org/wiki/Humorism*

SNOT Licence
*otm.wustl.edu/for-industry/tools/snot-16-20-22*

Hospital Bogeys
*sciencedaily.com/releases/2012/11/121108151728.htm*

Snot Toothpaste
*ncbi.nlm.nih.gov/pubmed/25344244*

Humming for Health
*atsjournals.org/doi/full/10.1164/rccm.200202-138BC#_i5*

Big Nose Picker
*oddrandomthoughts.com/picking-your-nose-will-make-it-bigger*

Death by Bogey
*telegraph.co.uk/news/uknews/3566273/Man-dies-from-picking-his-nose.html*

Dinosaur Snot
*youtube.com/watch?v=alFm3QI2TLY&t=4385*

Ape Snot
*nationalgeographic.com/news/2015/08/150822-animals-apes-science-noses-health-dogs*

Giraffe Snot
*discoverwildlife.com/animal-facts/mammals/facts-about-giraffes*

Dog Snot
*vcahospitals.com/know-your-pet/why-do-dogs-have-wet-noses*

Whale Snot
*sciencedaily.com/releases/2017/10/171010133930.htm*

*shop.whale.org/collections/merchandise/snotbot*

Escar-goo
*medicalxpress.com/news/2019-11-snail-slime-science-mollusks-medicine.html*

*wikipedia.org/wiki/Snail_slime*

Sea Snot Shooters
*fieldmuseum.org/blog/spiderman-worm-snails-discovered-florida-shipwreck*

Romantic Slug Snot
*wikipedia.org/wiki/Mating_of_gastropods*

Frog Snot Medicine
*news.emory.edu/stories/2017/04/flu_frogs_jacob_immunity*

Sneeziest Animals
*nationalgeographic.com/news/2015/06/150627-animals-science-elephants-anatomy-sneezing*

*anapsid.org/sneeze.html*

Snot Polite
*Elias, Norbert.* The Civilizing Process, p. 117-125

Snot Statistics
*uselessinformation.org/nose*

*bbc.com/future/article/20150202-why-do-we-pick-our-nose*

Gross Grave
*thevintagenews.com/2017/04/25/the-mourners-of-dijon-one-of-the-most-remarkable-examples-of-medieval-statuary*

Napoleon Bogeypart
*pastnow.wordpress.com/2015/04/16/april-16-1815-hobhouse-sees-napoleon*

*pastnow.wordpress.com/2015/04/30/april-30-1815-more-napoleon-nose-picking*

*dailymotion.com/video/x754eiu*

Minister Mucus
*youtube.com/watch?v=6VaP1HB7Vew*

*thelondoneconomic.com/politics/iain-duncan-smith-picking-his-nose-and-eating-it-is-just-a-taste-of-things-to-come/04/09/*

*express.co.uk/news/politics/1240456/Jeremy-Corbyn-Labour-Party-leader-Parliament-picking-nose-video*

Her Royal Sinus
*metro.co.uk/2014/05/16/the-monarchy-has-bad-habits-too-you-know-the-queen-leads-the-ranks-of-the-right-royal-nose-pickers-4730719*

*stuffdutchpeoplelike.com/2012/02/20/picking-their-noses*

Synthetic Snot
*Official Gazette of the United States Patent and Trademark Office: Trademarks, November 27, 2007*

Snot Swimsuit
*navytimes.com/news/your-navy/2017/02/12/expanding-slime-has-captured-the-imagination-of-navy*

Robo-Bogeys
*warwick.ac.uk/newsandevents/pressreleases/artificial_snot_enhances*

Nose Picking Day
*scgsmcovers.blogspot.com/2018/04/banners-international-nose-picking-day.html*

Nose Climate
  *academic.oup.com/jnci/article-abstract/23/5/979/939359*

Blowing It in Europe
  *home.bt.com/lifestyle/health/wellness/how-to-blow-your-nose-in-public-according-to-an-etiquette-expert-11364224823997*

Blowing It in Asia
  *lifehacker.com.au/2017/08/all-the-ways-youre-secretly-being-rude-abroad*

Nose Picking Tours
  *mentalfloss.com/article/585429/easter-island-statues-threatened-by-tourists*

Scientist Snot Jokes
  *youtube.com/watch?v=PqXOlfwlVag*

Superstar Snot
  *news.bbc.co.uk/2/hi/entertainment/7796991.stm*
  *en.wikipedia.org/wiki/Matshishkapeu*

The Nose Pickin' Song
  *Partridge, Eric*, Dictionary of Catch Phrases

It Really is Gross
  *psycnet.apa.org/record/1995-36836-001*
  *businessinsider.com/boogers-snot-eat-nose-unhealthy-science-virus-bacteria-2019-1*

How to Stop
  *ncbi.nlm.nih.gov/pmc/articles/PMC6207173*
  *verywellfamily.com/how-to-stop-nose-picking-in-preschoolers-2764835*

# Who writes this stuff?

**M.D. WHALEN** (writer)

He was always the kid who sat in the back of the class scribbling stories and cartoons. Later he sat in front of the class scribbling stories, when he should have been teaching! Now he writes full time in the back of his house, and has published many books under other names. He also enjoys cycling, world travel, and making rude noises in different languages.

**FLORENTINO GOPEZ** (artist)

His career began at age 6, when his cousin discovered him drawing on the ground with barbecue sticks. He wisely switched to pencils and pens, and has since worked all over the world and won awards as an animator and illustrator. His guitar and ukulele playing are as funny as his drawing.

# Think snot is funny? Wait until you read about farts!

Did you know that girl farts stink worse than boy farts? Fish farts nearly started a war. How many farts do you inhale on a plane? Learn and laugh with the best-selling encyclopaedia of intestinal gas.

Dog farts, cat farts, nurse farts, kids in prison for farting, farting queens and ministers, ancient fart tales. Plus how to fart in other languages. Complete your fart education with volume two.

# Know the facts?
# Now read the stories!

Can Willy and Peter defeat the evil clowns and save all humanity from ex-*stink*-tion with Weapons of Mass Flatulation?

Willy and Peter blast their way into space. But do they have enough gas in their guts to repel an invasion of flatulent bean creatures from Uranus?

# JOIN US!

## FARTY FARTERS CLUB*

## FARTBOYS.COM

*Even girls are allowed!

Printed by Amazon Italia Logistica S.r.l.
Torrazza Piemonte (TO), Italy

16417935R00082